THIS BOOK BELONGS TO :

CW00411571

••

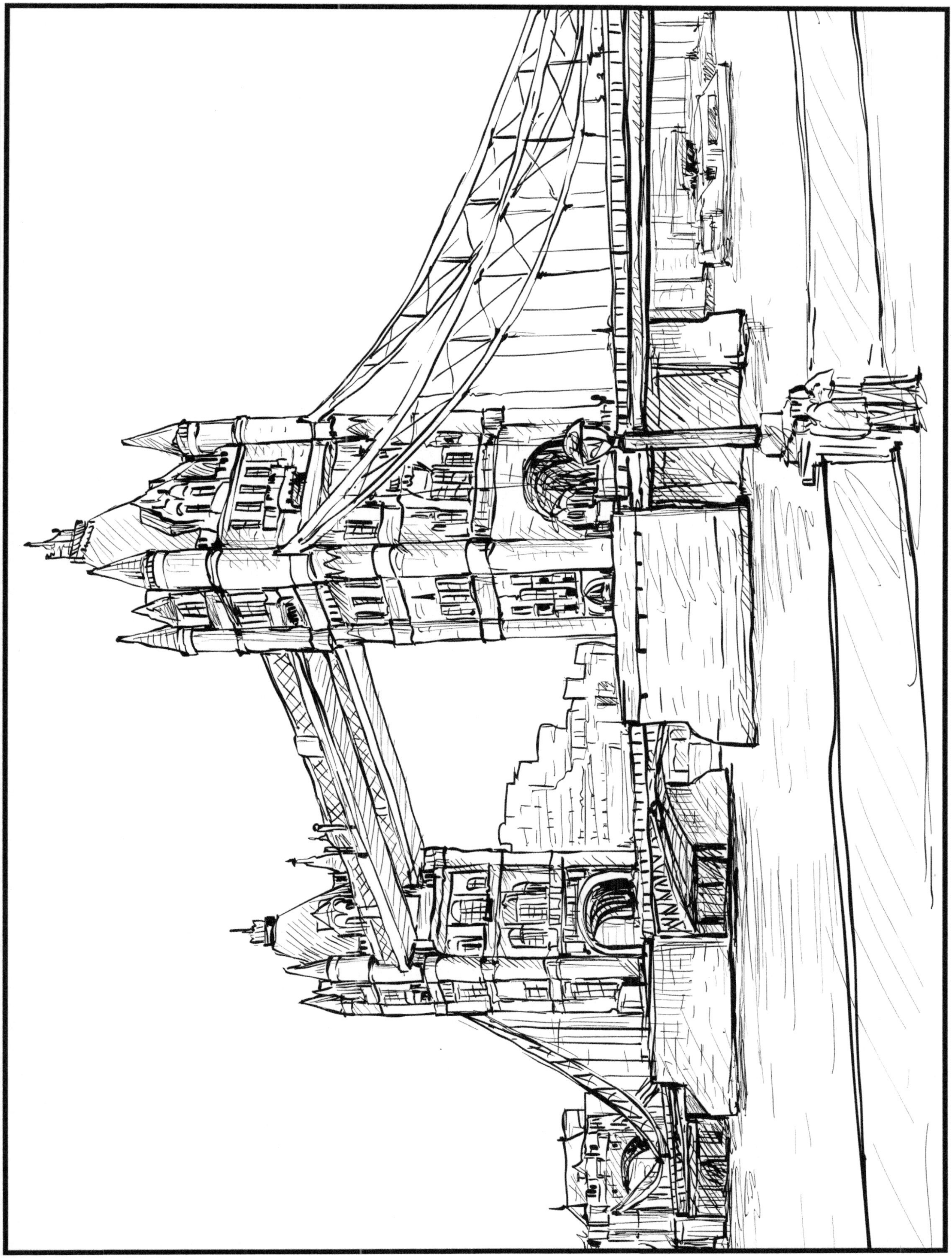

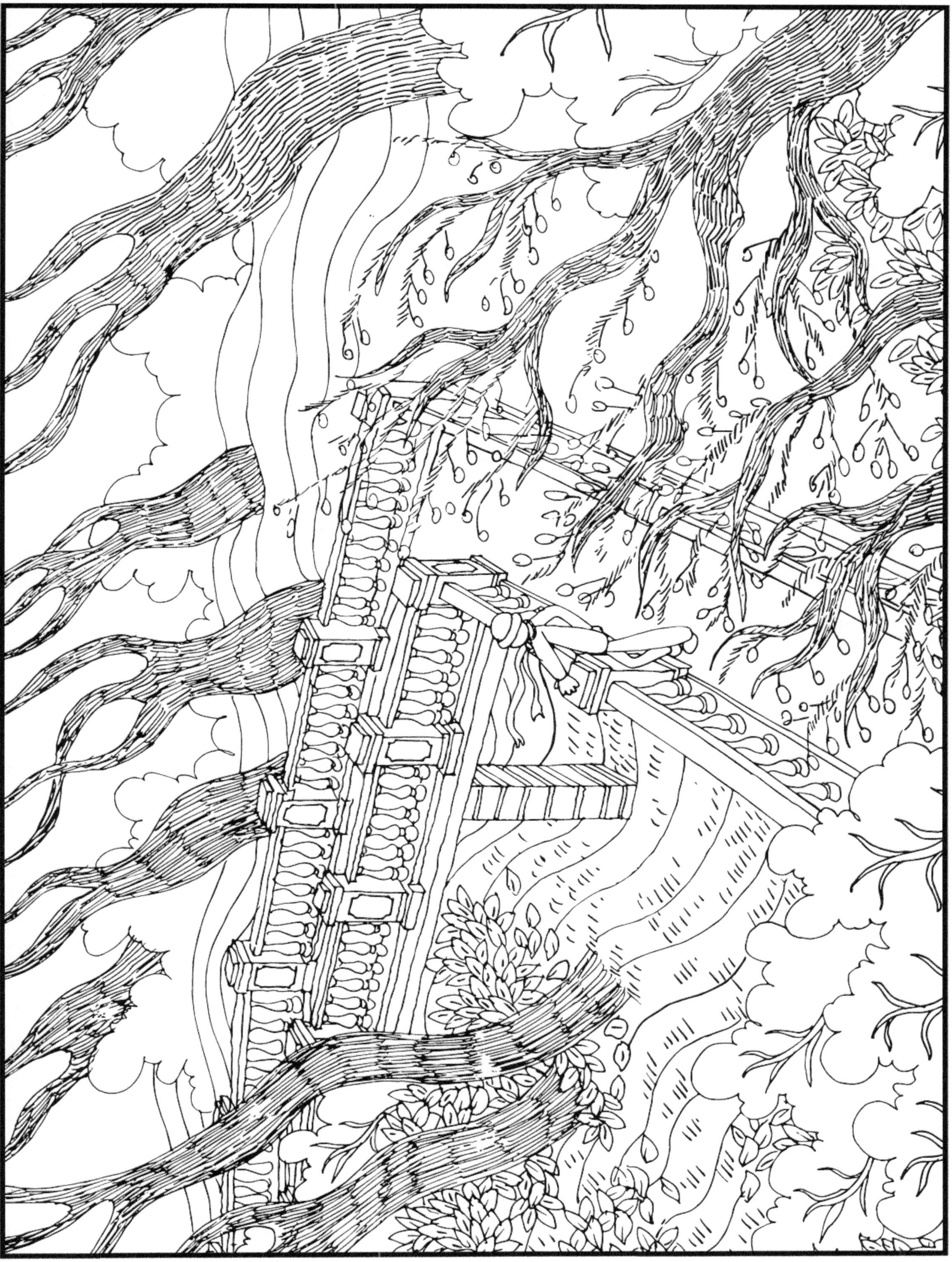

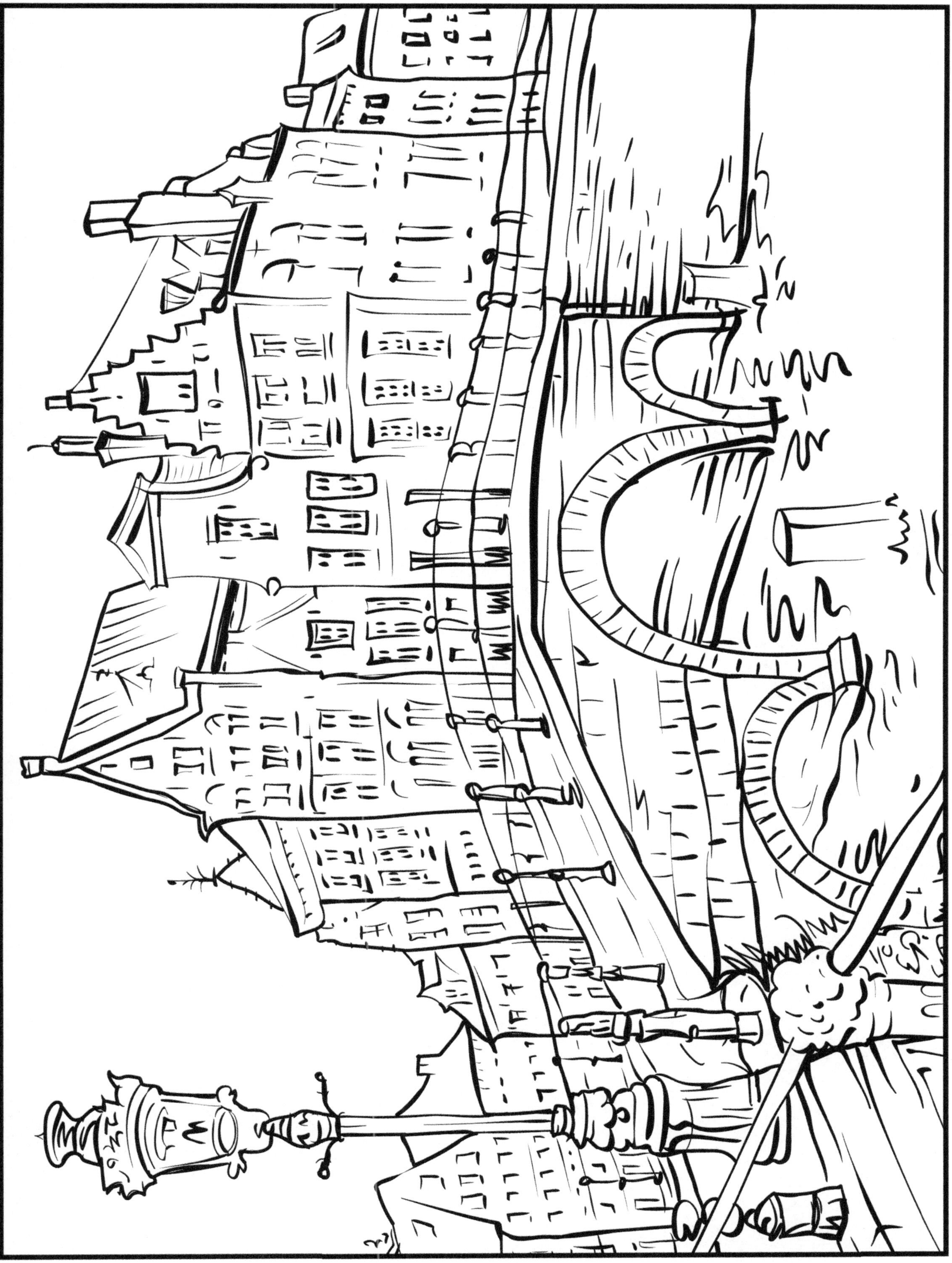

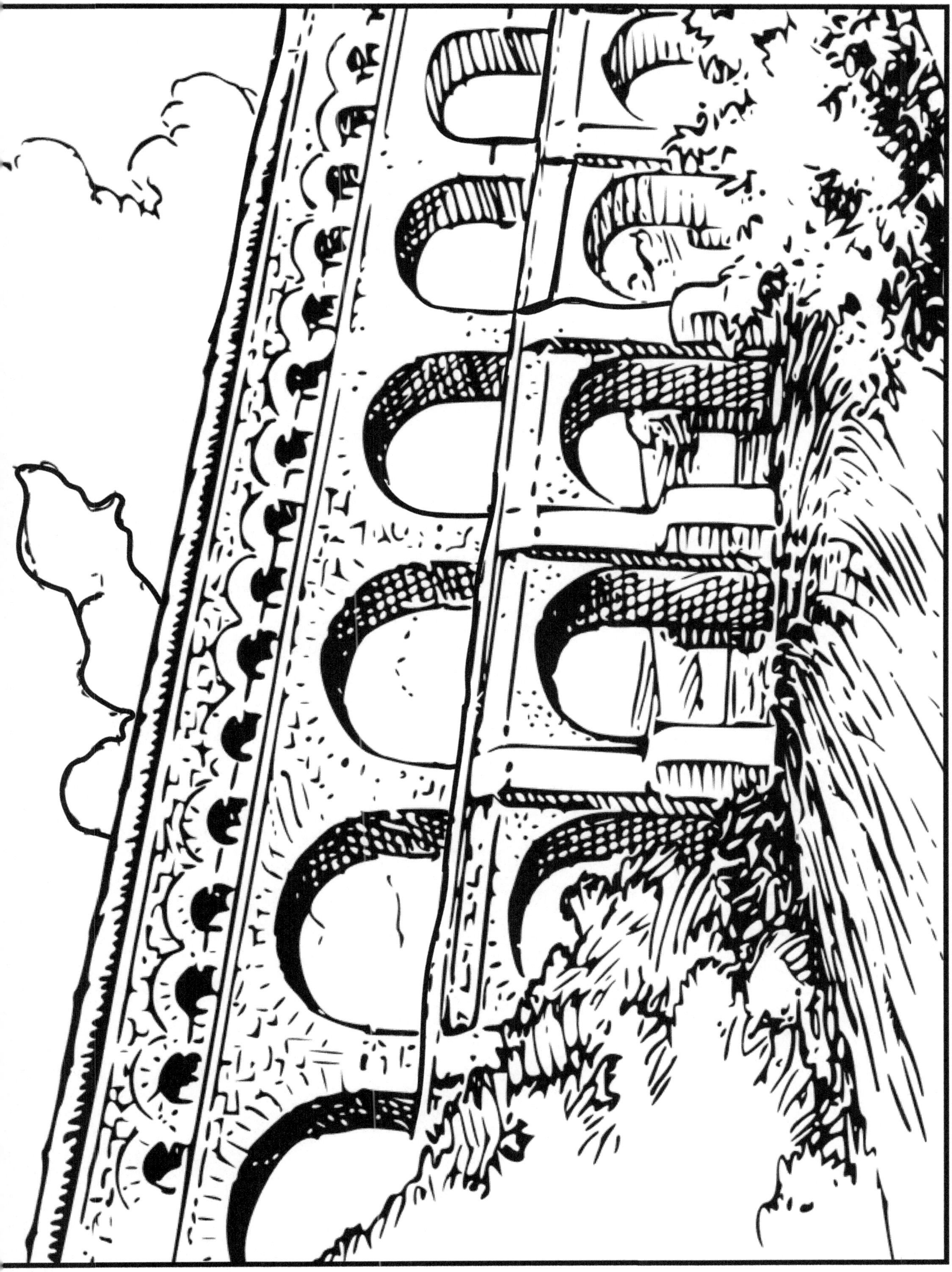

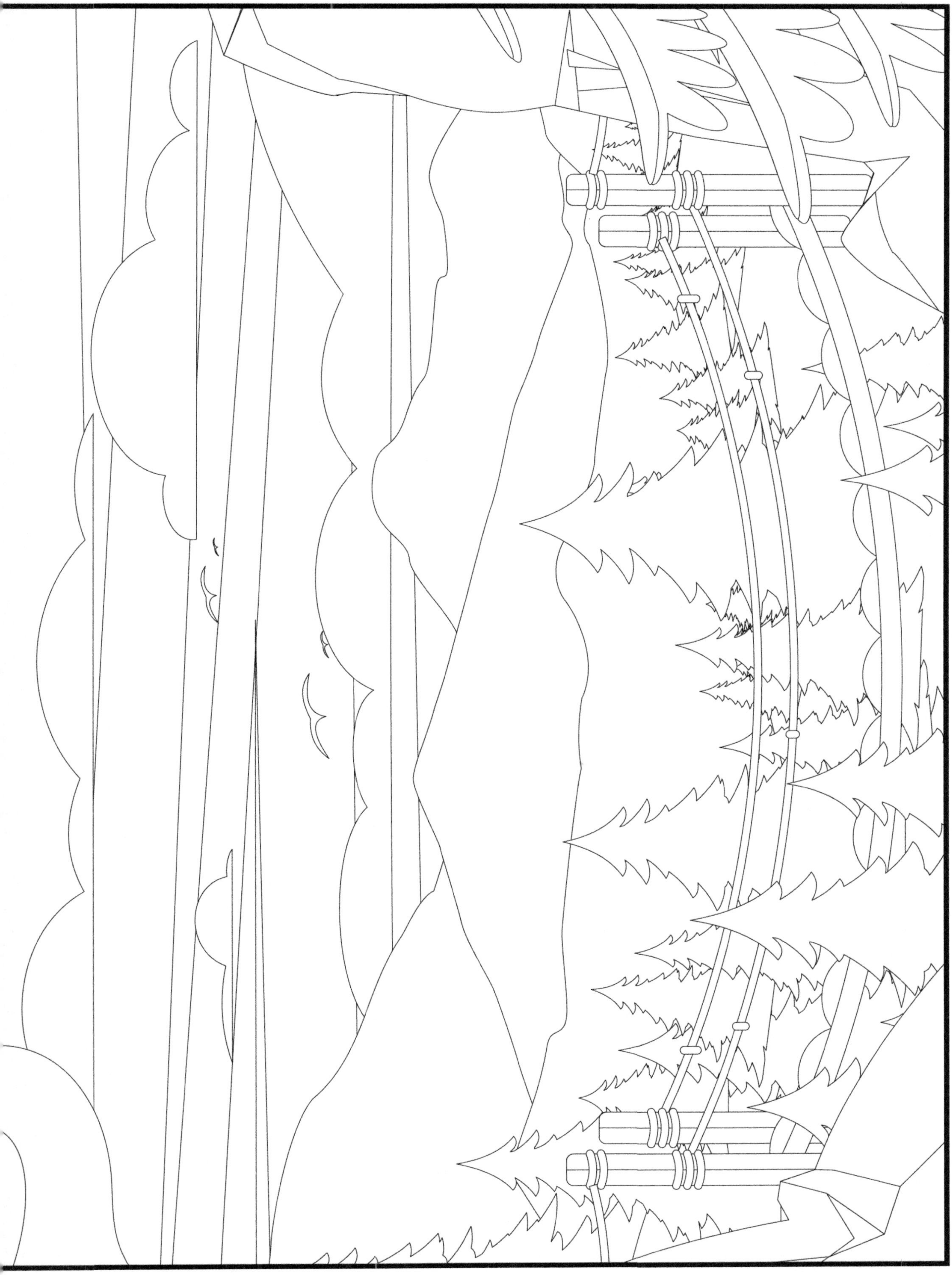

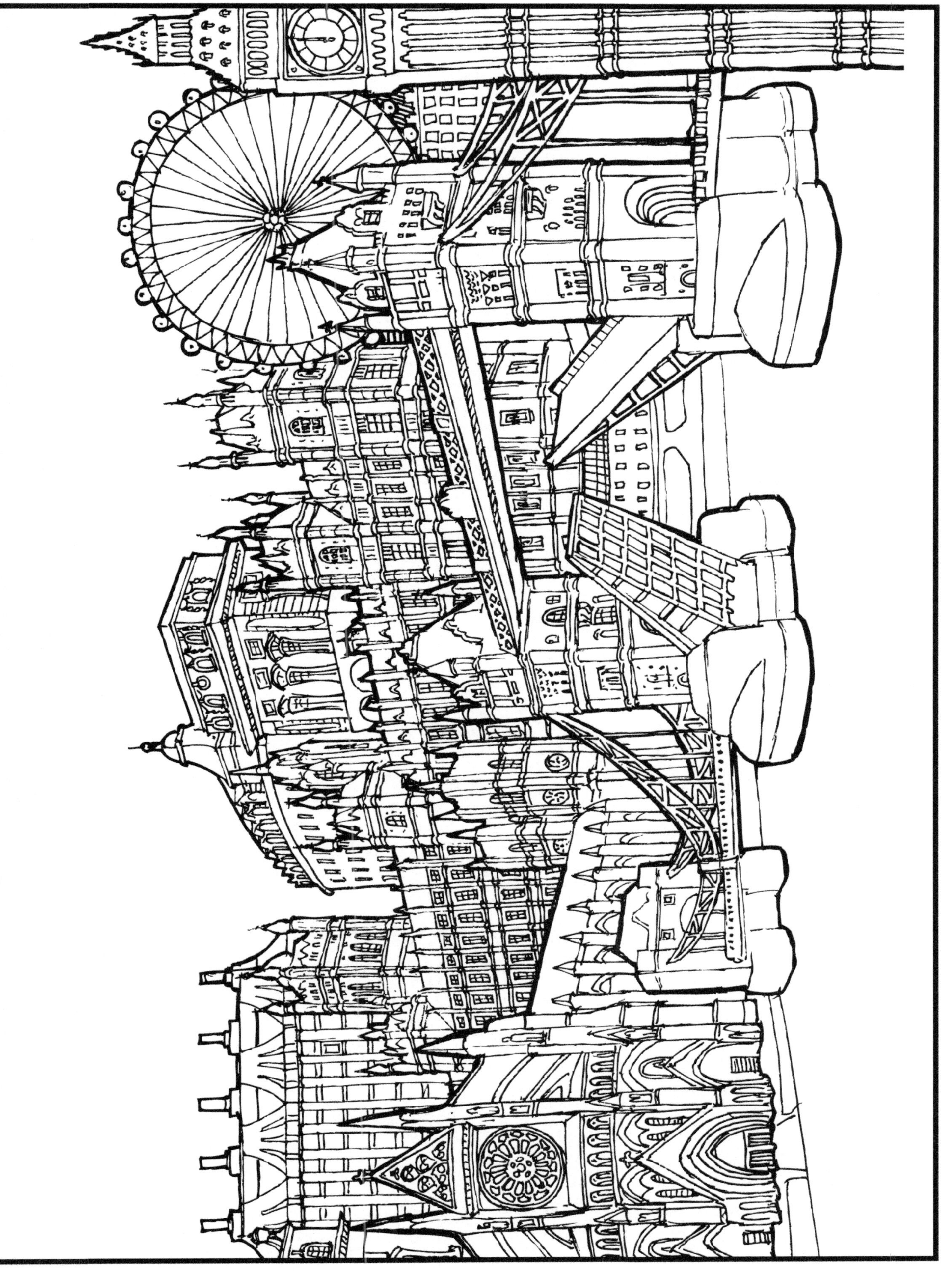

Printed in Great Britain
by Amazon

11244177R00038